So You Want To Be a Soldier

How To Get Started In Civil War Re-enacting

Shaun C. Grenan

SCHROEDER PUBLICATIONS

2003

Front Cover: A future re-enactor contemplates being a Civil War soldier, and how to get started, then is transformed as a Union soldier. *(Photo by Patrick A. Schroeder)*

Back Cover: Three Confederate re-enactors in full field gear represent typical Southern Civil War soldiers. *(Courtesy of Carl Zambon)*

Cover Design: Maria A. Dorsett Schroeder

Published by
SCHROEDER PUBLICATIONS
131 Tanglewood Drive
Lynchburg, VA 24502
www.civilwar-books.com
civilwarbooks@yahoo.com

Printed by
Farmville Printing
Farmville, Virginia

ISBN-1-889246-19-0

This book is dedicated to First Sergeant Thomas R. Grenan of the

78th New York Volunteer Infantry,

the *Lochiel Cameron Highlanders.*

You are not forgotten.

TABLE OF CONTENTS

AUTHOR'S ACKNOWLEDGMENTS

I would like to thank a few people who have helped make this book possible. First of all, I appreciate Historian Patrick A. Schroeder for his introduction and he and his wife, Maria Dorsett Schroeder, for editing, formatting and publishing my work. Secondly, I have much gratitude to my mom, Irene Grenan, for all the Civil War books and library trips as a kid, and my dad, Jack Grenan, and Nancy for the trip to Gettysburg for the first time.

I would also like to thank my bud Kyle for helping me get here, as well as Nate and Curtis for enduring the 12-hour drives. I would also like to thank my coworkers, and Bern Atkins, and Beth Atkins for helping me in my new hometown. Lastly, many thanks go out to Sylvia and Britta for their proofreading suggestions. You all have made this project achievable.

Shaun Grenan (lying on the ground) and friends of the 114th Pennsylvania Infantry, Collis' Zouaves. *(Collection of Shaun Grenan)*

PUBLISHER'S ACKNOWLEDGMENTS

I would like to express thanks to Shaun for the work he put into this project and his patience with getting it published. Carl Zambon sent numerous photos to assist us with this project. I'd also like to thank my parents for helping me when I was getting started in re-enacting, for supporting and encouraging my ambitions. My father often drove me to events, before I was legal to drive, and gave up many a weekend for my hobby.

I'd also want to pay tribute to my grandfather, Robert R. Astle, a navy veteran of World War II (U.S.S. Kephart and PCE(R) 850). Though he has passed on, he loved to attend a good Civil War re-enactment as a spectator and take photographs, some of which are included in this book.

Special thanks to Jason Jamerson who posed for the cover of the book and Maria Dorsett Schroeder, my wife, who put her valuable time into formatting and editing the book, and designing the cover. I am grateful to the 5th New York Volunteer Infantry, Duryée's Zouaves, re-enacting group, for taking me under their wings when I was starting out, and for encouraging my participation and love of history.

Patrick Schroeder (third from the left) and friends pose on the movie set of "Love Letters." *(Collection of Patrick A. Schroeder)*

INTRODUCTION

I started re-enacting in 1982 when I was 14-years-old, and it would have been such a benefit to have a book like Mr. Grenan has written in my hands. The numerous questions that flood the mind when getting started in the hobby are all answered right here. I was constantly on the phone asking members of my unit where to get this or how to do that. They were invariably helpful, but all the time and money expended in phone calls could have been better spent if I only had a published guide to set me on the proper course.

Most of us like to share how they got started in re-enacting, and this is how it began for me. I was born in Virginia, but grew up in New York and from childhood had a fascination with living history demonstrations at battlefield parks and historical sites. We made several ventures to Civil War territory hitting places such as Gettysburg and Fredericksburg, but in New York it was all Revolutionary War related. When I was 13, we moved to Virginia and we went to the annual re-enactment of the Battle of New Market in May 1981—I was hooked. I wanted to be a part of a re-enactment and wondered just how to go about it. At my young age, I mistakenly thought I would have to start my own group and began sending letters to historical sites inquiring just how to do this. Needless to say, I did not have much success. The following year, I knew exactly what I had to do—go to the event at New Market and find a unit to join. I talked to several units—Union and Confederate—all were helpful, but one group in particular attracted my attention. I spotted an elaborately painted recruiting sign for the 5th New York Infantry, Duryée's Zouaves (American soldiers that wore the French style Zouave uniform with ornately trimmed jackets, baggy red pants, and a tasseled fez cap). I chatted with one of the Zouaves, Charlie Klein—who looked like he had stepped out of a black and white Matthew Brady photograph, with a waxed moustache. He gave me a recruiting brochure and told me about the unit, and I wanted to join there and then. Why the Zouaves? As was the case with many a Civil War recruit, it was a combination of the unit's reputation and the flashy uniform they wore. The Zouaves were regarded as the toughest, bravest soldiers of the era, and I wanted to be a part of a unit that intended to honor and recreate those colorful warriors. At that time, the 5th New York was one of the leading units of the day and still remains active today. But I had questions, many questions. What exactly do I need? How do I get my gear? Where do I get it? Who do I get it from? How much does it cost?

That was just the start. It took some time to get these questions answered. Fortunately, unit members were able to piece together enough uniform parts and equipment for me to attend a unit event held at Manassas Battlefield National Park, where the 5th New York held a ceremony at the original regiment's monument, and performed demonstrations for the public. Even after attending a few events, the questions continued to arise. How do I know when I'm shot?—That's a favorite one people like to ask re-enactors. What do I need to bring for food rations at an event? How do I make hardtack? What about drill and loading a musket? The questions seemed endless. It was several years before I got all those questions answered. But thanks to this volume, the new re-enactor recruit will not have to go through all that—the answers are all here.

Mr. Grenan explores and addresses all those questions that bedeviled me in those days as a re-enactor "fresh fish"—how to learn where Civil War events are held, determining an appropriate organization to join, the different types of Civil War units, getting equipped, weaponry, the various types of events, the methods of going into battle, and the activities back in camp. He even gives some basic information on drill and the steps for loading and firing a musket. The material is presented in an easily read and understood manner.

Civil War re-enacting has a long history, in fact, the post Civil War United States Army, would occasionally "re-enact" Civil War battles, though they shouldered the weapons and wore the uniforms in use at the time. Re-enacting today has something for everyone, though this book focuses for the most part on becoming a soldier. There are civilian, sutler, surgeon, chaplain, signal corps, and a host of other impressions. For some, re-enacting is a chance to get away from the job or home and lose themselves in the past. For others, it is something they can do with family or friends.

For the younger generation, re-enacting instills a sense of history and offers a chance to learn history something more than what is taught in the classroom. The belief that "history is boring" quickly fades on a re-enactment battlefield or amidst a living history demonstration. Re-enacting offers excellent opportunities for young people. When I was in my teens, I was always doing yard work around town to get money to buy my gear and uniforms. On the weekends, I was off to an event—it didn't leave a whole lot of time to get into trouble. In fact, re-enacting will offer many opportunities. Travel—participants will get to visit many areas of the country to take part in different events as well as touring battlefields and historic sites. Several years ago, my unit traveled to France and Belgium where it performed numerous demonstrations, and we were honored guests of the town of Hirson. Movie making—as the public fascination with the American Civil War continues, many re-enactors have had the chance to work on movies and television programs such as *North and South Part II*, *Glory*, *Gettysburg*, and *Gods and Generals* and documentaries such as, *Civil War Journal* and *April 1865*. Books—many books include photographs of re-enactors in a book or on the cover. Job opportunities—the performing of living history demonstrations at a historical site or park could lead to future employment at such a place. For me, as a writer, my re-enacting experience has facilitated my writing as I have a better understanding of what Civil War soldiers went through, and on a small scale, what they had to endure. And no matter Confederate or Federal, a certain bond develops among re-enactors.

Re-enactors also develop a reverence for the past and take an interest in preserving the history of our nation. Many battlefields and historic sites have been saved from development through the support and interest of the re-enacting community.

More than anything else, I consider re-enacting and living history demonstrations a tribute to those Civil War soldiers who were willing to lay their life on the line and the many who gave up their lives. It is a wonderful way for us to pay homage to those gallant soldiers no longer with us, so their deeds and sacrifices will not be forgotten.

I hope to meet you on the field some day.

Patrick A. Schroeder
Lynchburg, Virginia

FOREWORD

I believe the most common question asked of a re-enactor, after "Aren't you hot?" is, "How do I become a re-enactor?" Becoming a Civil War re-enactor is easy and quite rewarding. The hobby of Civil War re-enacting is constantly gaining in popularity, thanks to movies, television, and the internet. Once interested in the hobby, a person can get hooked. There are certain steps to take when investigating the hobby, as well as when undertaking it. Not all of the steps may be necessary for each person, but there are some basic guidelines to know. Following these steps is a sure way to join the ranks of the ever-growing hobby of Civil War re-enacting.

It is my hope that you will find this book helpful for your own re-enacting endeavors and experience.

Shaun C. Grenan
Gettysburg, Pennsylvania

Thousands of spectators gather to witness the 125th anniversary of the Stacking of Arms Ceremony at Appomattox Court House National Historical Park *(Collection of Patrick A. Schroeder)*

FIND AN EVENT

A vital step to becoming a Civil War re-enactor is to attend some re-enactments or living history presentations as a spectator. There are several ways to go about finding an event to attend. There are a few magazines and newsletters out there specifically for the Civil War re-enactors, such as the *Camp Chase Gazette, The Courier, Civil War Traveler, The Watchdog,* or the *Civil War News*, that have a wealth of information on the Civil War as a subject, as well as a hobby. They list the major upcoming events for the year, and are great to use as an aid for planning a trip to include several events. They can be found online, such as at www.civilwartraveler.com, or at sutler shops, battlefield parks, or sometimes at your local newsstand or bookstore.

The local tourism bureau or historical society is also a good place to go for information about upcoming events. Many times, historical societies have a number of re-enactors involved in it. As members, they will not only be able to inform you about upcoming events, they can also give you information on their units as well. A re-enactor is always recruiting! The local travel/tourism bureau is a good place to check as well, as it is their job to be up-to-date with all the local events. Some tourism bureaus or visitor centers at historical towns or sites publish free monthly booklets that list some information on the area, as well as a schedule of events for that month.

Another way to learn about upcoming re-enactments or living history demonstrations is to call the national, state, or private park associated with that battlefield (if there is one). They are visited by thousands of tourists a year and are up-to-date with the latest happenings that may perk the interest of any tourists to their area. Often, re-enactments are held close to the original battlefields, many of which are now National Parks, such as Antietam, Gettysburg, and Shiloh, to name a few.

ATTEND AN EVENT

When you attend an event, there are a few pointers to remember. Foremost, enjoy the event! If you are going to find a unit, pay attention to the different things that go on to make up the event, as well as to the various units that you see in action. There are certain things that have been known to catch one's eye. The most obvious eye-catcher is if a unit wears a flashy or varied uniform. There are hundreds of different uniforms available, some conservative, some gaudy. Just like during the Civil War, some units gained recruits through distinctive dress, such as the Zouaves or the Chasseurs.

Another aspect that may interest you is how well drilled a unit is, or how well the officers command the men in the field. You want to make sure that the unit you choose to join is led by competent officers who can put their men smoothly through the maneuvers in battle, as well as on the parade ground. A unit that looks good and marches in good order is an attractive unit to a prospective re-enactor.

Be sure to note how safe a unit is. Pay attention to things like how they load and fire their weapons and how they handle swords, bayonets, etc. See if a unit "plays fair" during a battle re-enactment. Do they take their fair amount of hits? Do they follow the actions of the rest of their army, or are they a group of cowboys endangering themselves and others? Do they acknowledge their foes of that battle after a hard-fought engagement, or do they form up and march straight back to their camp?

Find out different impressions portrayed by the unit. Do the re-enactors come across as real soldiers, or as re-enactors? Do they all portray the same exact impression or are they a group of individuals, with quirks and flaws, like actual soldiers? Do they willingly welcome spectators to their camp and answer questions? Are they friendly and looking for new members, or do they exhibit "a *don't bother us*" aura? Are they knowledgeable as to the basic history of the unit they portray, or can they at least lead you to someone who can answer a question that they may not be able to answer?

When visiting an encampment, freely ask questions. That is the easiest way to gather information about the hobby. Veteran re-enactors are ready to help a new recruit with a piece of advice they have picked up through the years. A little question and answer session is the perfect way to judge the character of the group you are courting. Are they friendly and personable to you, or are you treated as a nuisance? Are they nice to

Confederate and Federal troops assemble prior to re-enacting the Battle of Cedar Creek, Virginia. *(Collection of Patrick A. Schroeder)*

you from the start, or only after you say that you are interested in joining? When visiting a prospective unit, it is also a good idea to take down contact names and addresses, pick up flyers, collect business cards, and get e-mail addresses from different units. This is not only a good way to make contacts in the world of re-enacting, but it is a great way to meet new people and make new friends! It is always good to have lots of friends in the re-enacting scene, as sometimes your unit may not attend an event, but you may be able to fall in with a friend's unit for that weekend.

Visiting an encampment is also a good way to see the different uniforms, weapons, accoutrements, cannon, etc., up close, which may answer some of the questions that you had. Most re-enactors are quite cordial, and do not mind letting a prospective member try on a uniform coat and/or accoutrements, and in some cases, may even run them through a little bit of drill to give them a taste. Often, once the "bug" sets in, the prospective member is hooked. This also helps a spectator see if they can make the transition from observing to participating. Many times, all a unit needs do is hear that illustrious question, "How do I become a re-enactor?" and all the members are running to their tents to fetch their extra gear. Pretty soon the potential recruit is geared up, just like the rest of the unit.

They might then run him through some drill with the rest of the unit, and possibly, if he handles it well enough, take the fresh fish out on the field for the next battle! Often times, that is exactly how a unit gets its new members, so they are always on the look out for that person shifting from foot-to-foot at the edge of camp, just waiting to hear *the* question.

A final pointer for when you visit a re-enactment is to make sure that you visit the different camps of *both* armies. You may have your heart set on Union infantry . . . until you see how nice the guys are in that Confederate artillery unit and vice-versa! If you visit the various camps, you will get to see many different groups out there, as well as the different branches of service. There are more than just infantry, cavalry, and artillery. Many people are surprised to learn about the Signal Corps, hospital stewards, chaplains, Sanitary Commission, civilians, and various other aspects to re-enacting. There is something for everyone. This is also a good way to dispel the stereotypes by seeing for yourself how similar the soldiers of the North and the South really are, and were. It is pretty eye opening to realize how it often was brother against brother during the Civil War. It is important to take this precept to heart.

Scene in a Federal camp at Shiloh, Tennessee. *(Collection of Patrick A. Schroeder)*

FIND A UNIT

Today, one of the best ways to get in touch with re-enacting groups is via the internet. There are literally thousands of websites online for the prospective re-enactor to peruse. Nowadays, most units have a website to make it easier for others to learn about their unit and to help recruit new members that may not otherwise have discovered their organization.

A good subject to search for online is "sutlers." Sutlers originally were entrepreneurs who followed the armies and set up tents for selling items to the soldiers that they could not get from the military, typically at exorbitant prices. Today's sutlers set up their tents at re-enactments and sell new and used items needed and used for the re-enacting hobby. There are many different types of sutlers, each specializing in different areas, so browse around to get an idea for the different prices on the equipment. One sutler may sell canteens for a good price, but charge an arm-and-a-leg for a hat. Sutlers' websites are also a good place to see the different equipment and merchandise available for purchase. Maybe you didn't know what a *tompion* was, or were wondering what exactly a *frog* has to do with a bayonet. Sutlers are usually good about answering e-mails and letters about the various pieces of equipment, in hopes of a sale.

Many times, sutlers also have a mail-order catalogue that you can request which lists more items that they carry than are shown on the website. Sometimes these catalogues contain sale items or packages that are only available through the catalogue. These catalogues often have photographs of the items too, as opposed to the listing of equipment that can be found online. Sutler websites have favorite link pages as well, which can link you to the websites of various other Civil War organizations and re-enactment web pages. Also, if time and distance permit, visit a sutler shop in person. This way, you can try on various uniforms and accoutrements, and have an expert there to answer any questions that you may have about what they sell. Many sutlers are re-enactors themselves, so they carry with them all the know-how of the hobby, as well as of the business. Sutler shops often have recruitment posters displayed from the various local unit as well, or a large grouping of business cards at hand. This is a great way to see what units are located in your general area. You may even be invited to join the very unit that the sutler is a member of (which might also give you a nifty discount on gear that needs to be purchased)!

Another good resource online is what is known as a *web ring*. A web ring is a group of sites that concern a specific topic or genre that is linked together in a ring. There are web rings out there for both armies, as well as all the branches of each army. Or, you can just look up "re-enacting" using the search engine of your choice.

Fifers and drummers play for the spectators. *(Collection of Patrick A. Schroeder)*

CHOOSE A UNIT

After all of that, you should have a wealth of information and choices at hand. You should have a unit, or at least a branch of the army, chosen. Sometimes choosing a unit may be automatic; some people are just a Yankee or a Rebel at heart. Others may identify with a "famous" unit from their state or city. Maybe they found an outfit with which their ancestor served during the War. Whatever the path you take, remember to take your time! It's not always best to join the very first unit that approaches you about becoming a member; you may end up stuck in a regrettable situation. Take the time to consider a couple of different units, and to ask them all the same questions to get their various responses (kind of like an interview). Ask other units about your prospective unit. There may be a bad reputation associated with that unit and you may want to avoid them! Most re-enactors will give you an honest answer when inquiring about a unit's reputation.

A large part of choosing a unit is location. Will you have to drive four hours to get to a monthly unit meeting, or are they held twenty minutes away? Some units are spread through a few states, but they have a central location where they can converge for their events. This makes it convenient for all the members. Again, the local historical society is a good place to check, for they often have members whom re-enact. This is the time to pull out all those business cards, names, addresses, and phone numbers that you collected at the different events!

Another good way to choose a unit is to read more about the Civil War. Read several books on specific battles, and there will always be vignettes of bravery of a few certain units. It may be the gallant deeds of a color-bearer shaking his fist defiantly at the approaching enemy, or the admiration of a lone soldier climbing over a wall to bring a last drink to the dying soldiers of the enemy. Some units may seem interesting for the fact they were so casualty prone! Most units ended the war with far fewer men that they began it with, and many were consolidated with others because of shortage of manpower. By the end of the war, some regiments were just a handful of tired, battle-hardened veterans. And again, some people just have to go for the flashy uniform with all the colors and the finery. There are re-enacting outfits that can fit any persuasion. If you read about a unit that you would just *have* to join if it exists, chances are it does! When all else fails, check the internet.

A good contact when researching the existence of, or joining of, a certain unit would be the Umbrella Organizations that most units are members of. These organizations are groups of units that camp, form up, and fight together. They try to make the hobby safer, as well as better organized. This is also a way to make sure that enough soldiers show up at a re-enactment. Some contacts for the major Umbrella Organizations are listed as follows:

1st Division Army of Northern Virginia
Bob Tolar E-mail:
Jtolar1@cox.net

3rd Regiment Army of Northern Virginia
Rick Britton E-mail:
RHBritton@aol.com

5th Regiment Army of Northern Virginia
Duffie GL Miller E-mail:
Cog17va@starband.net

Artillery Reserve
Mike Bealing
E-mail:
artilleryreserve@blazenet.net

Breckinridge Battalion
Archer's Brigade
Longstreet's Corps
Irish Brigade Association
P.O. Box 3495
Wayne, NJ 07474

Dept. of the South (U. S.)
Commander James Permane
E-mail: jpermane@aol.com
Chief of Staff, Jeff Grzelak
E-mail: 17thConninf@cfl.rr.com

First Federal Division
Brig. Gen. C. Warnick

120 Hilltop Meadow
Frankfort, KY 40601-9213

Hood's Texas Brigade Association
c/o The Harold B. Simpson
Confederate Research Center
Hill College
P.O. Box 619
Hillsboro, TX 76645

Liberty Rifles
Web site: www.libertyrifles.org
Andrew Dangel
8417 DT Loch Raven Boulevard
Towson, MD 21286

Longstreet's Corp
Jim Mauphin E-mail:
GenJWMaupin@aol.com

The Mifflin Guard
Andy Siganuk
413 New Brooklyn Road
Williamstown, NJ 08094
Scott Washburn E-mail:
shwashburn@erols.com

1st Missouri Infantry Battalion, C.S.A.
Colonel Doug Moody
Col1stmo@aol.com

The National Regiment
Dave Valuska

P. O. Box 265
Phoenix, MD 21131
Fax: (410) 692-9544
E-mail: valuska@kutztown.edu

Northwest Civil War Council
P.O. Box 898
Mulino, OR 97042

**Provisional Army of
Confederate States (PAC)**
Greg Bair
Email: bair@shentel.net

**Re-enactors of the American
Civil War**
Monte Sidenstricker
38 Linda Drive
Oroville, CA 95969

**United States Volunteers
(USV)**
Aide in Charge: Reg Wirth

6 Timber Lane
Hatboro, PA 19040
E-mail:
rwirth@mail.phila.k12.pa.us

**United States Volunteers
Cavalry (USVC)**
Craig Beachler
E-mail:
Beachler@oasisonline.com

Vincent's Brigade
Wayne Wolff
5904 Pt. Pleasant Drive
Baltimore, MD 21206
E-mail:
Wayne.W.Wolff@bge.com

The Western Brigade
Chris Abelson
2500 Bonita Drive
Waterford, MI 48329

A mixing of Federal and Confederate troops after one of the annual Gettysburg re-enactments. *(Collection of Patrick A. Schroeder)*

RUMORS

Now that you know some of the steps on how to become a Civil War re-enactor, some rumors and myths should be addressed and dismissed. Many people are scared away from the hobby because of the myths that tend to plague it. One of the myths that puts a stigma on re-enacting is that you have to be a drinker to be a re-enactor. Some re-enactors themselves pass this around. Nothing could be further from the truth! There are units out there that may go by this stereotype, but those are the units you learn to avoid joining or even fraternizing with. Most units are quite respectable, yet still allow freedom to their members.

A second myth is that you must attend every event that your unit is invited to participate in. There are certain events that a unit will ask all of its members to try to attend, but there are no mandatory events. Part of being a hobby is that participation is voluntary. Most people's schedules do not allow them to be free to make every event all year long; therefore, members attend events as their individual situations allow.

The third and fourth myths in re-enacting go together; that you must be hard-core and that re-enacting is serious all the time and like the actual military. Campaigns re-enacting, or hard-core re-enacting, is the style most closely associated with realism. Hard-core re-enactors strive to relive history by experiencing all the same hardships as the Civil War soldiers did. They carry all of their possessions, food, etc. with them for the whole event and often sleep on the bare ground with nothing between them and the stars. There is a sect of re-enacting that follows this path, but the majority of re-enactors are a bit more mainstream in their impressions and attitudes. The degree of authenticity varies, depending on the individual units themselves. You will always be able to find a unit that is at your chosen level of realism (for lack of a better word). As for the level of seriousness, again, that depends on the specific unit. There is always going to be a serious side to re-enacting because of the respect, honor and dignity associated with the hobby.

The point of the hobby is not only to educate, but also to honor the memories of the soldiers who fought the Civil War. The safety issues in re-enacting also encourage everyone to pay close attention to how they handle items like weaponry and black powder. The safety of the participants should always be the number one priority at an event. After the battle, however, the veil of seriousness is lifted, and the jokes, songs, and stories can be heard around every campfire.

The fifth rumor in re-enacting is that every re-enactor is a walking encyclopedia or historian who spends all their time not spent re-enacting reading volumes of Civil War literature. True, every re-enactor is an amateur historian in their own right, but you pick up bits-and-pieces of history here and there. Many re-enactors, therefore, are weekend historians. You will learn more as you attend events over time. Some re-enactors enter the hobby with only a small amount of Civil War knowledge to their credit, as it is not necessary to know all the history to participate in the hobby.

The last rumor to address is that there is animosity between Northern and Southern re-enactors. Re-enactors come from all parts of America, as well as from other countries, and are parts of both armies. The sectional differences that brought on the Civil War are not, and should not be, a part of re-enacting, but beware of the bad apples out there that will take things to extremes. These days, the sectional tensions are part of a show put on for the spectators at living history events. It is not unusual to find Northerners donning gray and Southerners wearing blue.

Artillery pieces crown a ridge prior to battle. *(Courtesy of Carl Zambon)*

GETTING EQUIPPED

Now that you have chosen an army and a unit, it is time to get equipped. The three basic units' uniforms to address are Infantry, Cavalry, and Artillery. First, the different types of uniforms for the Infantry are discussed. The Infantry uniforms are broken up into seven different categories: Union Volunteer, U. S. Regular, Zouave, Chasseur, various Union regimental dress, Confederate Volunteer, and various Confederate regimental uniforms.

One of the easiest uniforms to acquire is that of a *Union Volunteer* soldier in the Union Army. This is the basic uniform that is seen in all the paintings and movies. This uniform consists of a pair of sky blue colored kersey wool pants (*trousers*), a dark blue four-button sack coat (*blouse*), and a kepi or a forage cap. A pair of brogans or Jefferson bootees would complete the outward appearance of a volunteer in the Union Army. Now remember, variations *always* existed. Some men wore the nine-button frock coat that regulations called for. In Army regulations, the sack coat was to be worn for fatigue duty, and the frock coat was to be worn in the field or on dress occasions. Eventually money, material, and the weight of carrying an extra coat made the sack coat useable for every occasion. As for headgear, many men brought with them hats from home, or purchased civilian style hats. The forage caps issued to the men did little to protect the soldier against the elements; so many men adopted the slouch hat. In the western theater, the slouch hat was more widely adopted than in the eastern theater, where the forage cap and kepi were the predominant headgear of the Union infantryman early in the war, at least through 1863. Check with your organization for uniform specifications and irregularities from the prescribed Army regulation dress. Some volunteer organizations, especially early in the war, had their own uniform for the unit, but this was often replaced with the regulation dress after the initial clothing wore out.

The garb of a *U. S. Regular* soldier differs from that of a volunteer soldier. A Regular was a soldier who had enlisted in the Army before the War began or during the War enlisted for National, as opposed to state, service. In theory, though not always in practice, the U. S. Regulars wore the dark blue wool frock coat with dark blue wool trousers. They were also to wear the model 1858 Hardee hat, with the forage cap or kepi for fatigue duties. The Regulars did not always have the leeway with regulations that the volunteer soldiers did—they were the professional soldiers.

Two soldiers wear the uniform of the 114th Pennsylvania Volunteer Infantry known as Collis' Zouaves. *(Collection of Shaun Grenan)*

The *Zouaves* were soldiers who based their attire totally or partially on that worn by the French-Algerian troops of the mid-1800s. They, in turn, had based theirs on a native Algerian tribe, the Zouaoua. The French Zouaves distinguished themselves during the Crimean War (1853-56). There were American Zouave regiments serving in both sides during the Civil War. The basic Zouave uniform was designed for comfort and mobility. The trousers were baggy and loose fitting. They gathered at the knees with gaiters or leggings, to secure the lower legs. These were often, in turn, covered with leather greaves, called *jambiéres*, just below the knee. The Zouave jacket was a short jacket with rounded edges, a low rounded neckline, and distinctive and colorful trim and designs called *tombeaux* on the jacket front. The men usually wore a vest beneath the jacket, or had a false vest front stitched to the jacket so that they appeared to be wearing a vest underneath their Zouave jacket. The headgear of the Zouave was quite distinctive, for it was usually a fez with a long tassel hanging down the back or side. Some units even wore a large turban over their fezzes, but this was principally for dress occasions.

A member of the 14th Brooklyn wears a Chasseur uniform.
(Collection of Patrick A. Schroeder)

The *Chasseur* uniform was the official attire of the French light infantry. At one point, there were plans for outfitting all of the Union soldiers with Chasseur dress, and over ten thousand were imported. The French uniforms, however, did not fit the larger framed American soldiers. Therefore, chasseur uniforms were given out to a few specific regiments as rewards for their skill in drill or for their bravery on the battlefield. Many pre-war militia units on both sides were outfitted in Chasseur uniforms.

There were also various Union regimental uniforms that were worn by units who kept their distinctive dress throughout the war. These regiments were often identified by these uniforms. They took pride in their distinctive, and sometimes flamboyant, garb. The *Iron Brigade*, for example, was always defined by their high top, black felt Hardee Hats and frock coats. Some of the men dropped the larger, heavier frock coat that they were originally issued, however, and wore only the four-button sack coat, but the men always kept their distinctive black hats. The Confederate soldiers were known to have referred to the Iron Brigade as the *Black Hats*. Another regiment with distinctive headgear was the *Pennsylvania Bucktails*. The Bucktails were known for their superb marksmanship, and most members had the tail of a deer adorning their slouch hats or forage caps. A final example is the 79th New York Infantry *Cameron Highlanders*. This regiment went off to war with full Scottish regalia, including bag-pipers and kilts. These men eventually conformed to the same uniform as the majority of United States Volunteers, but some held on to reminders of their heritage, such as the checkered Glengarry cap, which they wore with their regulation uniforms. Some men held on to their kilts and Scottish regalia to use for dress occasions as well. The 39th New York Infantry, the *Garibaldi Guard*, were known for their red shirts and for adorning their hats with green feathers, as well as the European uniforms worn by some of their officers, who professed to have served in the armies of Europe. There were over 10 different languages spoken in this one regiment alone! The *Garibaldi Guard* eventually drew to regulation dress.

A *Confederate Volunteer* infantry uniform often appears to be mix and match. Many times, it depends on the time period in the war you are portraying. Early in the war, many units could follow the prescribed regulations, and were well clothed. Supply problems sometimes limited what a unit received, and much was made up for by procuring civilian items and dying them the familiar butternut color.   A common Confederate infantry uniform may be composed of gray or sky-blue kersey-wool trousers, a gray wool or jean-cloth jacket, and a slouch hat.

(Left) **A Confederate infantryman rushes from the protection of a bombproof ready to do battle.** *(Right)* **Bag-pipers of the 79th New York Volunteer Infantry, know as *Cameron's Highlanders.*** *(Collection of Patrick A. Schroeder)*

Again, check the specifics with your unit first. Some units were known to wear more of the butternut-colored uniform than of the gray variety. Also, some units, such as the Maryland regiments, were known to be supplied with kepis throughout the war. The southern states also had their share of finely dressed militia units early in the war, but after a year or so in the field, many of these units discarded their finery for more practical wear.

Three Confederate foot soldiers rest on a stone wall prior to battle. *(Courtesy of Carl Zambon)*

There were also various Confederate regimental uniforms. Some units held on to their special uniforms for a number of years, while others converted to the easier-to-supply-styles of gray or butternut uniforms. The Confederacy had their share of famous units. The *Maryland Guard Zouaves* were a unit with short blue Zouave jackets with red trim, blue semi-baggy trousers with red trim, and a red kepi with a blue band. A pair of white canvas leggings completed the outfit. This unit was organized mainly from some of the better-off families in Maryland. One of the most well known of all Confederate units was the *Tigers Rifles*. These men wore a red fez with a red tassel. For recruiting purposes early in the war, some members wore a straw hat inscribed with a slogan. (This was before they were issued Zouave uniforms.) They also wore a dark blue Zouave jacket with red trim, baggy Zouave trousers with blue ticking, gaiters, and striped socks. *Coppens' Zouaves* wore a red fez with a blue tassel, baggy red Zouave pantaloons, and dark blue Zouave jackets with the color of the jacket's trim depending on the company. The *Alexandria Rifles* even wore green frock coats with green trousers and a green kepi. Variations abounded in both armies. Confederate uniforms are known for a more homespun look, and many re-enactors pride themselves on how original their clothing appears.

A Federal cavalryman. *(Collection of Shaun Grenan)*

Cavalry uniforms can be just as flashy, or just as serviceable as their infantry counterparts. Cavalry dress can be broken down into three basic categories: Union Cavalry, Confederate Cavalry, and Dragoons. The

Union Cavalry also wore the sack coat, sky-blue trousers, and the forage cap or slouch hat. The trousers had a reinforced seat for the mounted men. Some men wore a short-jacket with the yellow trim of their service branch. This type of jacket was called a roundabout or a shell jacket. The Union cavalry had its showy units too. The *3rd New Jersey Hussars* wore a visorless forage cap, a triple-breasted coat, and an orange lined cape, or talma. This uniform was based on the *European Hussars*, a type of light cavalry, and earned the 3rd New Jersey the nickname the *Fighting Butterflies*.

A Confederate cavalryman with a guidon. *(Collection of Patrick A. Schroeder)*

The intrepid *Confederate Cavalry* was and is a very appealing branch of service. The exploits of raiders such as John S. Mosby, John Hunt Morgan, and the adventures of J. E. B. Stuart, Wade Hampton, Joe Wheeler, Turner Ashby and Nathan Bedford Forrest will keep people entertained forever. An example Confederate cavalry uniform is composed of a civilian hat with feathered plume, a gray short-jacket, gray trousers, and knee-high boots. Depending on things such as the state the unit is from and the year of the war being portrayed, the attire will vary. Regulations existed, but only to an extent. A legendary Confederate cavalry unit was the *Sussex Light Dragoons*. This unit wore high blue kepis with yellow trim and "S.L.D." on the front. They also wore dark-blue trousers and a blue frock coat. Owing to confusion on the battlefield, the blue frock coat was dropped in exchange for a large, gray double-breasted shirt with a large pocket on the side. The Confederate cavalrymen west of the Mississippi were more singular in their garb. Many of them wore uniforms provided by loved-ones at home. The variety of homespun uniforms were widespread in the Confederate armies in the latter stages of the war.

Dragoons were a type of cavalry that could fight on foot. Both sides used dragoon style units throughout the war. Dragoons in the United States Army were done away with just before the war, and converted to cavalry, but some of the former dragoons still wore their orange-trimmed, short jackets in their new regiments. They would ride to the scene of battle and then dismount to act as skirmishers or infantry. This is the style of fighting that General John Buford employed to make his cavalry units more effective when facing infantry during the Battle of Gettysburg, and Nathan Bedford Forrest utilized this strategy in the western theatre as well. Most cavalrymen and mounted infantry dismount during fights of battle re-enactments. This way, they get to participate more in the engagement, although several large-scale cavalry battle re-enactments have been organized over the years.

The *Artillery* uniform of the Civil War soldier is the basic infantry uniform with a few variances. Some men preferred the shorter shell jacket to the sack coat. These short-jackets would have red piping—the branch or service color for the artillery is red. The red trim is less prevalent in the Confederate uniforms as opposed to their Union counterparts. Many Confederate artilleryman wore the six-button sack coat, and North Carolina issued butternut, six-button sack coats to some of their men.

There are uniforms for other impressions, such as *Signal Corps*, *Pioneer Corps*, and *Hospital Staff*, but they are the same as other uniforms previously described, with a few variations, such as different color and style chevrons, with branch of service emblems. The Confederate Ambulance Corps often wore a red band around their hat with the words "Ambulance Corps" on it. This served to identify the actual members of the Ambulance Corps from shirkers and stragglers.

(Above) **A group of Confederate artillerymen in the field.** *(Collection of Shaun Grenan) (Below)* **Federal artillerymen fire their cannon.** *(Photo by Robert R. Astle)*

(Above) **A navy man visits a tavern with an infantry captain.** *(Below)* **A Vivandiere (a woman wearing military garb who sometimes accompanied her Zouave regiment) takes the field with her unit.** *(Collection of Patrick A. Schroeder)*

(Left) **Re-enactors of the 54th Massachusetts Volunteer Infantry rest by the ocean prior to their assault on Fort Wagner.** *(Right)* **An officer and soldiers of the 54th Massachusetts Volunteer Infantry.** *(Collection of Patrick A. Schroeder)*

EQUIPMENT

Now that we've covered the uniforms used by each branch, the next topic to discuss is the accoutrements used by each branch. The accoutrements are broken down into three sections; the basics (the must have), secondary (ones to acquire down the line), and optional.

For infantry, the basics are what make up the majority of your gear. The *canteen* is a very important piece of equipment. This vessel carried water (and occasionally, other liquids) for the soldiers. They come in many different shapes and sizes. The basic union canteen is an oval shaped canteen with a wool cover, usually of gray, sky blue, or dark blue. The straps are leather or cloth. Late war canteens had concentric rings pressed into them giving them the name "bull's-eye canteens". Confederate canteens come in a much larger variety. You will see captured Union canteens, tin drum-shaped canteens, wooden drum-shaped canteens, glass-lined leather canteens, and more. There were also private- purchase canteens available to the soldiers. Some of these had a filtering system to take the impurities out of the water. These filters could keep dirt out of the water, but did not keep germs out. Many soldiers shortened the strap of their canteen to make it ride higher up, making it more comfortable to carry. The leather strap is adjustable, but the cloth can be cut and re-sewn at the appropriate length. Many re-enactors tie a knot in their cloth strap, which is quicker and easier for those who cannot sew. Though some re-enactors say that this is incorrect, there are examples of original canteen and haversack straps, as well as photographic evidence, showing that knot tying was employed at the time.

The next items discussed are known as the *Leathers* in re-enacting. The leather items (the belt, cap box, bayonet scabbard, and cartridge box) are black for the Union forces, and they are black or a russet brown color for Confederates. The first item is the belt. This piece holds your gear down, and you can also attach a cartridge box to it in the absence of a sling. Some Confederate belts are known to have been tarred or a painted canvas. The plates or buckles come in a variety of shapes and sizes. The basic Union plate is a lead-filled brass oval with "US" stamped on the front. However, be sure to check with your unit, because some regiments had belt plates issued by their state, which had a state designation such as "SNY" (for State of New York) stamped on the front. Confederate buckles and plates range from the simple, such as the basic frame buckle (almost like the ones on modern belts), to imported British snake buckles, with a clasp of interlocking hooks shaped like snakes. On the re-enacting field, it is very common to find an upside

34

This Confederate infantry corporal sports a North Carolina belt plate. *(Courtesy of Carl Zambon)*

down "captured" "US" plate (which is said to look like SN and stand for *Southern Nation*) and the basic "CS" or "CSA" plates. Some Confederate units also had state specific plates, such as the Pelican embossed plate worn by some Louisiana units.

The second part of your leathers is the *cartridge box*. This item is self-explanatory. The cartridge box holds ammunition, as well as the tools for cleaning and maintaining your weapon. The cartridge box was either worn on a sling over the shoulder, or on the belt. The cartridge box is to lie on or over your right hip. More Confederates are supposed to have worn the cartridge box on the belt as opposed to using a sling because of their lack of materials. The cartridge box usually contains two tins for the Union forces, and one large tin for the Confederate forces. These tins held 20 rounds of ammunition on the top of the box, with extra rounds underneath. These tins were designed to protect the wearer in case of an explosion in the box. They were constructed to force the explosion outward, away from the body. Some re-enactors do not use them, since they tend to be a hassle, and on rare occasions, cut up your hands when reaching for a cartridge. You can also fit more cartridges in the box without the tins in them. Therefore, these tins are not a necessary item to purchase, unless required by your unit.

The third piece of the leathers is the *cap box*, or cap pouch. This attaches to the belt in the front of the body, to the right of the belt-plate. This small leather box holds the percussion caps used in firing your rifle. There is a piece of lamb's wool on the inside of the box to keep the caps from spilling out. This wool sometimes becomes unglued. Some re-enactors intentionally remove this piece of wool. It is really a matter of personal preference. Be prepared to glue or stitch this piece of wool in a few times. In more authentic cap pouches, the wool will be stitched in.

The secondary items for an infantry re-enactor are next. The first secondary item is your *musket*. Most units give you up to a year to purchase this item, and have a spare rifled musket that you can use in the meantime. More information about muskets follows, in the chapter "Weaponry."

The next two secondary items go together; the *bayonet* and *scabbard*. There are two main types of bayonets used in re-enacting; the *Springfield* and the *Enfield* bayonet. They are made to fit their respective muskets. Both are socket bayonets that lock on the musket over the front sight, and both have a triangular shaped blade. The Springfield bayonet scabbard is attached to its frog by rivets, and/or stitching. The *frog* is the leather loop that attaches the scabbard to the belt. The Springfield scabbard is worn on your left side and rests at an angle pointing behind you. The Enfield scabbard hangs down from its frog, and it is not permanently attached to it. This scabbard is also worn on the left side, and hangs straight down making a 90-degree angle with the belt. Both scabbards usually have a brass tip on the end for safety purposes.

The fourth secondary item of the infantry re-enactor is the *haversack*. This cloth, tarred, or painted canvas bag holds rations, eating utensils and sometimes the Civil War soldier would include personal effects. The Union haversacks are predominantly painted or tarred black to make them water-resistant. The basic Confederate haversack is a cloth one that closes with buttons or a buckle. The Confederate haversacks were sometimes very colorful, for some are known to have been made from carpet! The haversack is worn on the left hip, under the canteen. It may be worn above or under the belt, depending on your personal preference. Many soldiers shortened the straps of their haversacks to keep them from hanging low and being too cumbersome. They used the same methods for this that they did to shorten their canteen straps. Usually, a haversack worn under the belt would not need to have a shortened strap, since the belt held it down.

The fifth secondary item is the *blanket*. This is a quite important item, especially if you are staying overnight at an event. It keeps you warm, keeps you dry, and can be rolled up and thrown over your shoulder to carry some personal belongings or extra clothing inside. This is what is known as a *blanket roll* or *mule collar*. There are various blankets available to the re-enactor. Some Confederate soldiers had quilts made at home and brought off to war with them. Others carried blankets made from rugs or carpeting. Some men tore a hole in the middle of a blanket so it could be worn as a poncho. Some Confederates were even issued captured U. S. Government Issue blankets, which were gray-brown with dark stripes on either end and a "US" stitched in outline in the center to mark it as government property.

The sixth secondary item is the *tent*. As with the rifle, most units will have an extra tent or two, or a fellow unit member will share his tent. This allows you time to procure a tent of your own. The basic tent is the *shelter tent*, or dog tent. Soldiers would carry a half of the tent, and would button it together with a fellow soldier's half. Then, they would have a tent big enough for two men. A third man could attach his piece as an end piece to keep out the wind, and create more room for a third man. In a more permanent camp, you would find larger   *A-tents* or *wedge tents*. These tents, being much larger, could hold up to six men.

A seventh piece of secondary gear is the *cartridge box sling*. This is usually mandatory in the Union army, except for the specialty troops such as Zouaves. Union Army regulations called for the black leather sling to have a circular brass plate, with an eagle stamped on it, placed on the strap. This proved to be a great target for Confederate sharpshooters, however, as the plate lay right over the heart. It was also just another piece of brass to shine for dress parade, and many men discarded it. The

Confederate sling, if one were used, could be either black leather, russet brown leather, painted or tarred canvas, or just plain cloth/canvas. The use of a sling with your cartridge box can make it much easier to reach when searching for a cartridge to load.

The final pieces of secondary equipment make up an important part of soldierly life—the *mess kit*. Napoleon is known to have said that "an army moves on its stomach." This statement definitely held true during the Civil War. A typical mess kit consists of a three-or-four-pronged fork, a large-headed round spoon, and a round-edged knife, a tin plate, and a tin cup. Some men used a half of a tin canteen as an impromptu plate. Some tin cups had a handle and a lid. These were larger than a drinking cup and could be used to cook with. These were known as *mucket*s. Others also used an old tin can with a homemade handle. Again, many units have extras that they will share until you acquire your own. Just prepare to get dish duty that night! This equipment would be carried in the haversack.

The optional equipment of a soldier are items that you do not need to have for every event, or may not need at all. These items help you to finalize your soldierly impression. If you plan to re-enact in the early spring or in the fall, when the weather is likely to be a bit uncomfortable, a good item to have is a *gum blanket* or a *poncho*. A gum blanket is a piece of canvas that is coated with vulcanized India rubber on one side. Sometimes, because of the lack of gum blankets, painted canvas blankets were issued. A poncho is basically a gum blanket with a slot in the center to put your head through. These make good ground cloths when setting up your tent. Regulations stated that gum blankets were for infantry and ponchos for use by mounted troops. These items have grommets on the edges so they may be used as impromptu shelter-half tents. The luxury of two gum blankets keeps body heat in and will help a soldier stay warm on the coolest nights.

Another good inclement weather item is the *greatcoat*, or overcoat. The Union soldiers usually had a sky-blue overcoat, but gray, black, and brown are known to have been issued because of a lack of sky-blue kersey. Confederate soldiers often wore captured Union overcoats to keep themselves warm, or used civilian overcoats brought from home. The Confederate government is known to have issued captured Union overcoats to its men. Confederate General Richard Garnett is said to have worn a blue overcoat, a remnant from his U. S. Army days.

Personal items are a good addition to any impression. Some common personal objects are books (Bibles were always popular),

A Confederate soldier wearing a greatcoat (overcoat). *(Courtesy of Carl Zambon)*

playing cards, a toothbrush and tooth powder, musical instruments such as harmonicas and Jews harps, pens/pencils and writing paper, a shaving razor, a pocketknife, cartes de visite (a type of Civil War-period photograph), dice, a comb, matches, handkerchiefs, etc. The soldiers carried almost anything you can think of, but reminders of home and family were most common.

A final infantry item is the *knapsack*. The knapsack saw heavy use by both Confederate and Union soldiers alike during the Civil War. Some soldiers discarded the bulky knapsack in favor of the blanket roll, but the knapsack was carried by men of both armies throughout the entire conflict. The Confederates were sometimes issued knapsacks captured from the Union Army. A knapsack is a large investment, and it is not a necessary item, so make this one of the last pieces of equipment on your "to acquire" list. The most popular types of knapsacks were the militia-style box knapsack for an early-war impression, and the double bag soft-pack, most frequently used after 1861. The box knapsack was a rigid painted canvas or leather knapsack that had a wooden frame on the inside to keep the smart look of the knapsack intact. The double-bag knapsack

A Confederate soldier in full field gear, with a knapsack, on a movie set. *(Courtesy of Carl Zambon)*

was a soft painted-canvas knapsack with two compartments: one for personal items, clothing, etc., and another for a folded up overcoat, blanket, poncho, etc.

Cavalry accoutrements differ from infantry in a few aspects. First, cavalrymen were expected to usually carry three different weapons: a saber, a pistol, and a rifle or carbine. And second, cavalrymen had a horse to carry gear, so things like a knapsack were not needed. They had saddlebags to carry equipment, as well as a saddle to attach equipment to.

The first basic accoutrement of the cavalry re-enactor is the *sword belt*. This carries the rest of a cavalryman's equipment. It is an over-the-shoulder, strap style sword belt of black leather. The sword belt is worn around the true waist, not low on the hips, like today's belts. To the belt, you attach a cap box, a pistol holster, a cartridge box, and a saber. The plate on a cavalryman's belt is usually a rectangular plate, but some Confederate belts would forego the plate and attach with a frame buckle.

Federal cavalry troopers. *(Collection of Patrick A. Schroeder)*

The next items are the *carbine cartridge box* and the *cap box.* The carbine cartridge box carried by the cavalryman often depends on the weapon. There were multipurpose carbine cartridge boxes available to the men. Check with the vendor you purchase your rifle or carbine for the appropriate cartridge boxes for your weapon. The cap box and cartridge box serve the same function for the cavalryman as they do for the infantryman. The carbine cartridge box was generally carried on the carbine sling, but sometimes attached to the waist belt. A pistol cartridge box may also be carried on the sword belt, but not all cavalrymen toted this piece of gear. Loading a pistol is hard enough, let alone doing it on a moving horse! Many cavalrymen would carry extra loaded cylinders for their pistol, or even extra pistols tucked into their belt. If you are dismounted and acting as infantry or as skirmishers, you will rely on your trusty carbine, and usually fall back before the enemy gets within pistol range. Unlike infantry cartridge boxes, cavalry versions have no buckles on the outside of the box. Get a box that is sized for the type of cartridges used by your carbine.

A canteen is just as important an item for the cavalryman as the infantryman. The styles and varieties of canteen for the cavalry match those of the infantryman.

The first secondary items of the cavalryman are the *saber* and *scabbard*. The sabers for cavalry impressions come in two main types— light and heavy. The light model 1860 and the heavy model 1840 were both carried in a wrought-iron scabbard with two rings on it to attach it to the sword belt. The scabbard is worn over the left hip. In many battles there were few or no sabers used by the cavalry. Therefore, a saber may be optional for some horsemen. Saber casualties were rare during the War, and like the bayonet, the saber was more commonly used to roast meats over the fire and to dig rifle pits. However, few re-enacting events are more fun for cavalry than a saber battle, so you will eventually want to acquire one and learn its safe usage.

The next secondary items of the cavalry re-enactor are the *pistol* and *holster*. The "hog leg" revolver holster was worn on the right side, with the butt-cover extending forward. The primary pistols of the cavalry during the Civil War were the Colt .44 Model 1860 Army pistol or the .36 caliber Colt M1851 Navy. Another pistol popular with re-enactors is the 1858 .44 caliber Remington six shot revolver. Again, a pistol cartridge box was sometimes used, but most men relied on extra loaded cylinders for their pistols, or an extra loaded pistol or two. Some well-armed cavalrymen even carried up to four loaded pistols at a time.

The fourth secondary item for the horseman is *gauntlets*. The basic cavalry gauntlets are buff-colored, and extend to the wrist. However, not all cavalrymen use gauntlets. Gauntlets were also not provided by the government, so cavalrymen had to purchase them on their own. A good pair of gauntlets will keep the straps of your horse tack from chafing your hands up, and will also help keep your grip.

Some other optional and secondary items for the cavalryman are the same as for the infantryman, such as the haversack, mess kit, rubber blanket/poncho, and overcoat. The cavalry was known to have the poncho more then the gum blanket. Also, the overcoat of the cavalryman is double-breasted, with a longer cape and higher collar than the infantry overcoat.

Personal items for the cavalryman mimic those of the infantryman as well.

There are some pieces of equipment that pertain only to mounted cavalry, such at the *carbine sling*, *saddle bags*, a *saddle*, *horse tack*, a *picket spike* and *rope* (to allow the horse to graze without straying), a *saddle blanket*, a *carbine boot* that attaches to the saddle (this holds the carbine muzzle in place while riding), and of course, the horse. The standard Union saddle used was the 1859 McClellan Saddle and the standard Confederate saddle from 1861-64 was the Jenifer. However, Confederates used some McClellan Saddles that were found in stock at the war's beginning, some were captured, and some McClellan copies were made by the Confederates. In 1864, the McClellan replaced the Jenifer as the "official" saddle of the Confederacy. Many Confederates used Texas Hope and Santa Fe saddles in the western theater. Plantation saddles were also used by Southern troops, and older army officers often used the Grimsley saddle. The unit you join will be able to provide you with an equipment list. All you need to do is ask.

The third role to address is that of the Civil War artilleryman. The basic equipment of the artilleryman is the easiest to acquire, and will use much of the previously discussed equipment from the last two impressions.

The primary item is, of course, the canteen. This, as you have seen, is a necessary item on the field. The belt and the haversack are the only other two pieces of basic equipment. These again, are the same style and configuration as those carried by the infantry.

The other equipment for the artilleryman is the same as that of the infantryman. Things such as a rubber blanket, wool blanket, overcoat, tent, mess kit, personal items, and knapsack can be used for this impression as well. These are the basic items of daily use that all soldiers would use. There are a few items that some artillery re-enactors carry, but not all. Some carry a sword and/or a pistol. These items are not necessary, and some artillery re-enactment units actually recommend *not* getting these items.

(Above) **Federal artillery in action at the re-enactment of the Battle of New Market.** *(Photo by Robert R. Astle) (Below)* **Confederate artillerymen rest against their cannon.** *(Collection of Shaun Grenan)*

WEAPONRY

The last portion of the equipment to discuss is the basic weaponry used by each branch of service. The main weaponry of the infantry in both Armies during the war was the Springfield and the Enfield rifled muskets. Before rifling (grooving the inside of the barrel that puts a spin on the bullet, allowing it to go farther, go faster, and be more accurate), battles were fought up close, often at 50 yards or less. The bayonet was a formidable weapon then, as were swords and pistols, because of the proximity of the battle lines. With rifling, however, men had weapons that could kill in excess of 500 yards. Some crack shots could hit an object up to 1,000 yards away! The model 1861 Springfield rifle musket was the standard arm of the Union Army during the Civil War. More than 700,000 of the 1861 model .58 caliber Springfield were manufactured during the war for the Federal forces. Many manufacturers copied the Springfield model 1861 to various degrees, and the armies issued thousands to both sides during the war. Many early war units carried smoothbore muskets that were converted from flintlock to percussion cap for the firing mechanism.

The second most widely used infantry weapon of the war was the British 1853 model .577 caliber Enfield rifled musket. Federal agents contracted over 500,000 Enfields from Great Britain, while Confederates purchased over 400,000. The Enfield was one of the best imported European guns of the Civil War. Many foreign arms were faulty, and were sold to the U. S. government because contractors knew that it was hungry for arms, and the government purchased them, often without regards to their quality and reliability. Many infantrymen went off to war carrying large, fierce looking bowie knives and privately purchased pistols as well. These weapons were soon discarded as useless as the men acclimated to the new style of warfare. Many Federal regiments required the men to turn in all non-issue weapons. Some units also replaced poor quality weapons after a large battle by picking up superior weapons off of the fields. At Gettysburg, entire regiments are known to use this practice to re-arm themselves.

The basic weapons of the cavalry, as previously stated, are the carbine or rifle (not to be confused with the rifled musket, which was longer and had a longer range). The most popular pistol of the war was the .44 caliber Colt Army model 1860. Some cavalrymen chose the .36 caliber Colt Navy model over the Army model, citing its "greater handiness." Over 200,000 of the Navy model were purchased during the war. Revolvers were issued only to cavalrymen and mounted light artillery. Some horse soldiers, however, also found their pistols to be useless in close-quarter combat, finding it hard to aim and load in the midst of a fight, and would rely upon their sabers; although guerillas, such as the men that served with Mosby, found the revolver more useful than the sabers. The main sabers used were the model 1860 Light Cavalry Saber and the model 1840 Heavy Saber, or the Dragoon Saber, nicknamed "Old Wristbreaker." The carbine was the essential weapon of the cavalry. The Union cavalry was more fortunate in their possession of a vast majority of the breech loading carbines. Most Confederate cavalry had to rely on muzzle loading carbines, sawed-off shotguns, and sometimes even rifled muskets.

Two of the most advanced cavalry weapons of the war were the Spencer carbine and the Henry repeating rifle. These Spencer and Henry rifles were also sometimes used by infantry. These guns came into use later in the war, with devastating effect. The .52 caliber Spencer held a seven-round magazine in the stock. The rounds were spring-fed into the chamber for firing. The .44 caliber Henry was one of the most technologically advanced weapons of its time. It had a 15-round magazine, and its lever action ejected the spent shell, loaded a new round into the chamber, and cocked the rifle all in one motion. The Henry was described by one Confederate soldier as "the gun the Yankees could wind up on Sunday and shoot all week."

The artilleryman also went off to war carrying wicked-looking knives and a variety of pistols. Some artillery officers were issued swords based on the Roman-style foot sword. This weapon was often exchanged or discarded entirely. Some artillerymen also carried short muskets (musketoons) or various artillery rifles and muskets. The main care of the artillery was their field pieces. The swords, rifles, and pistols were just more baggage to tote on the long march.

TYPES OF EVENTS

There are basically five different types of events when it comes to Civil War re-enacting: a Skirmish, a Re-enactment, a Tactical, a Living History, and a Parade.

A *Skirmish* is a small event. Usually skirmishes only involve up to one hundred re-enactors, often less. Many times a unit will contact some of its sister units and they will get together to put on a show for the weekend. Many times these are not for spectators, but are for re-enactors to get another chance to put on the wool, drill, camp out, and burn some powder. They often have elements of all the branches of service there, but not in force. These can take place just about anywhere, depending on the size of the event. Often times these are also drill weekends for a number of units to get back into the swing of things after a long winter of inactivity on the re-enactment front. This way the units will look good next time there is a crowd of people watching.

A *Re-enactment* is the most visited event. They can be all sizes. Some have been extremely large, like the 20,000 plus re-enactors that participated in the 135th anniversary of the Battle of Gettysburg. These events often bring spectators and re-enactors together from all over the country and world. Sometimes there are thousands of spectators that line up all along the field to view the battle, as well as peruse the various camps and sutler tents. These events are often filmed if they are anniversary events or large-scale events, and the videos can sometimes be purchased from sutlers through the mail or at a later event. The larger events always bring out the sutlers and provide good opportunity to pick-up some needed gear. Many of the larger anniversary events are held annually and they take place on or near the actual battlefields themselves. These battle re-enactments almost always fall on the anniversary of the battle, or on a weekend near the anniversary. These are great events to experience camp life since they are multiple-day affairs. Nothing beats an evening around the crackling campfire after a hard day's work on a spectator-surrounded battlefield. This strengthens and renews the bonds of brotherhood that gives re-enactors an opportunity to forget their regular lives, jobs, worries, etc. and live in an extraordinary period of our country's past. These are the moments re-enactors live for, not so much the battles, but the camaraderie. When there is no modern intrusions around, a re-enactor may experience what is often called a "bubble"—where the troops and atmosphere surrounding them easily lets them view scenes and have feelings experienced by an actual Civil War soldier, and no one wants this bubble burst.

A Confederate battle line delivers musketry fire. *(Photo by Robert R. Astle)*

A *Tactical* is the culmination of the re-enacting experience! Tacticals are for re-enactors only, and are not scripted like a battle re-enactment. A tactical is as close as you get to an actual battle in re-enacting. The generals take command of their respective armies, deploy their forces according to their plans, and basically fight it out. A tactical can take place anytime, day or night, and they are completely unpredictable (just like an actual battle). On one side of the field, your line may have been flanked, and your forces are getting raked mercilessly by enemy fire. On the other end of the field, however, you may have the enemy completely surrounded and are about to coax a surrender! A tactical takes place over all types of terrain and involves the element of surprise as much as luck—anything can happen. A tactical is usually a part of a larger weekend event.

A *Living History* is usually a small event. Living histories are encampments and scenarios set up for the public. Many times these events take place at museums, historical sites, schools, or campgrounds. They can include weapons firing demonstrations, hospital scenes, court martials, mail calls, firing squads, and various other scenes of daily soldier life. Living histories involve numerous question-and-answer ses-

Confederate infantry over runs a Federal artillery position. *(Photo by Robert R. Astle)*

sions with the public, and are generally more difficult than fighting a battle because of the amount of public interaction. Sometimes living histories are done in the "First Person," whereas most re-enacting is done in the "Third Person." Sometimes, these events call on a re-enactor to portray a specific character, be it an actual person or a made-up character. These interpretive events help one work on their impression and staying in character for an event. There are units that specialize in living histories, as opposed to battle re-enactments, and their impressions are first-rate. They are always in character, and never let the 21st century slip out. These events require you to brush up on your history—the history of your unit, as well as that of the Civil War and life in the 1860s.

The last event type, the *Parade*, is pretty much self-explanatory. A parade is a chance to put on your full-dress uniform, blacken your leathers, and polish your brass. It is basically a time to smile, look pretty, and get your pictures taken by hundreds of anonymous spectators. Just remember to walk in step with the guy in front of you, and watch out for those flowers the ladies throw (slippery little devils)!

(Above) **The 5ᵗʰ New York Volunteer Infantry, Duryée's Zouaves, march in the annual Remembrance Day Parade at Gettysburg, Pennsylvania.** *(Courtesy of Sharon A. Schroeder)* *(Below)* **Federal prisoners of war are held captive in a stockade during a living history event at Ballstone Mansion, Maryland.** *(Courtesy of Arnold T. Schroeder)*

(Above) **During a living history event at Appomattox Court House National Historical Park, soldiers and civilians recreate a famous photo taken by the Civil War period photographer, Timothy O' Sullivan.** *(Below)* **Civilian re-enactors pose in front of the historic Clover Hill Tavern at Appomattox Court House National Historical Park.** *(Collection of Patrick A. Schroeder)*

EVENT TIME

Here are some basic steps to follow, or pointers to remember when preparing to go to an event. The first thing to address, of course, is how you are going to get there. One of the best things you can do is carpool to an event. More often than not, someone in the unit will be passing near your residence on their way to the re-enactment, so it would not be too much trouble to stop by and pick up another member. Not only does carpooling save money and gasoline, but it is also the perfect way to get to know your comrades better. Veteran re-enactors always have some great stories and jokes that they love to tell you again and again—and carpooling is a great way to hear them. To new re-enactors, every story adds to the excitement, and may give them a piece of knowledge that they find useful in the upcoming event. Another important part about the trip to an event is that it is a great time to get psyched up. Nothing gets the juices flowing and the feet tapping like the sweet sounds of fife and drum! And, no, re-enactors cannot "carry a tune in a haversack," but nothing is more fun that crooning out the classic Stephen Foster songs or patriotic hymns!

The second step, naturally, is arrival and setting up camp. After you find your company street, pick a spot for your tent. Just remember the Army regulations for setting up camp. The first tent on the street should belong to the First Sergeant, and the remaining tents should be placed in a straight line based on his tent. Have some fellow members help you with your tent, and it will go up much easier! After you get your tent set up, make sure to help out the other members of the unit in setting up their weekend homes. Also, the officers always need help putting up their big tents, and that's what privates are for (or so the officers think)! After the other members' tents are up, try to fit all of your equipment inside your tent, all the while making sure that you have comfortable sleeping quarters that will keep you warm and dry. Some straw and a gum blanket rank up there with the softest of mattresses after a long day's fight!

After your little plot of ground is squared away and made into a cozy little home, there may be some free time. One good field activity is the rolling and filling of cartridges. You can buy pre-rolled cartridge papers, but it is not all that difficult to cut a paper into strips to roll your own cartridges with. Just make sure you do not put too much powder in them—you may need a powder measure. Also, make sure that you are using the correct grain powder—fffg or ffg work just fine. It is usually easier to make your cartridges at home, but you never really can have too many rounds. It is also nice when you can lend a few to a buddy who runs out in the heat of battle, or to the new guy who is at his first event. If you are low on cartridges or powder, make sure to purchase them early at an event, because they don't last long at the sutlers! A final cartridge rolling pointer: when closing up a filled cartridge, leave a lip or flap to grip with your teeth to tear. You can secure this flap by tucking it into a fold in the cartridge, or by using a glue stick to secure it to the side of the cartridge. This will also help keep you from losing your powder all over your cartridge box as it gets jostled around. It all depends on how good of a cartridge-maker you are and if you don't mind glue in your mouth along with the paper and the black powder! Make sure to pack your cartridge box nice and full of rounds before the first battle. This should usually last you through most, if not all, of the event. If you need help learning the proper way to roll and load a cartridge, ask a veteran re-enactor. They will have rolled and loaded hundreds or even thousands of cartridges before, and will gladly spare the five minutes of time it takes to pass on their knowledge of the art of cartridge rolling.

You will also want to make sure that your percussion cap box is loaded up and ready to go. However, do not overfill your cap box, or you will see those caps spilling out all over the field. You do want to have an ample supply at hand though, because of the percussion caps' tendencies to fall off of the nipple, as well as fall out of the cap box, sowing themselves like seeds in the field. If you squeeze the cap gently before placing it on the nipple of your weapon, it will fit more snug. Again, make sure to purchase caps early at an event if you need them, because they are bought up quickly after the first battle. Reminder: there is a piece of lamb's wool in the box to keep the caps in. Sometimes it works, and sometimes it doesn't. As fore-mentioned, it has tendency to tear out or come unglued. You will find re-enactors who go with the wool, as well as without. After a few battles, you will learn what is your personal preference.

Another piece of pre-battle equipment advice involves the bayonet. Sometimes, other re-enactors may advise you to use string to tie your bayonet in to your scabbard to keep from losing it. This may seem like a good idea at the time. However, when you need to remove your bayonet for drill, or for dress parade, or for musket inspections, it may seem to be more of a hindrance. It is really not a good idea to tie your bayonet to your scabbard. A better, as well as easier, safety measure is to layer your bayonet between your haversack and canteen. This will keep you from stabbing yourself, as well as your comrades in arms.

Always remember to stay hydrated! Drilling and maneuvering in wool uniforms in high temperatures can take a lot out of the human body. Locate the *water buffalo* (water tank truck), when setting up camp so it will be easy to find when it comes time to fill your canteen (or others if you end up with canteen duty). Make sure to have a full canteen when going into battle! The "*hurry up and wait*" adage for the military holds true even in re-enacting. A cool drink is always welcome while standing in line of battle under a hot sun. Most importantly, if you do not have a canteen, you will not be allowed to participate in the battle! This may not be true for all units, mind you, but it is a very good rule to follow. This is another case where safety of the participants prevails. Heat stroke from dehydration has occurred at re-enactments. It happens regularly when people do not drink enough water. Carbonated drinks just serve to dehydrate you more, and sports drinks are mainly sugar, so remember to stick to good ol' water!

Federal re-enactors rest near their stacked muskets prior to the start of a battle. *(Collection of Patrick A. Schroeder)*

FALL IN

A few hints to remember when gearing up:

- Always have a full canteen
- Always have a hat of some sort
- Bring a handkerchief
- Bring something to munch on

Wear a hat of some sort. Number one, it is part of your uniform. Number two, marching, fighting, or while just standing around, it can be detrimental to have the sun beating down on your head. Not only is it uncomfortable, it makes you sweat, and it can give you ferocious sunburn (and some re-enactors have more vacant scalp to get burned than others do)! A good hat can also keep the sun out of your eyes, and it is a good place to keep a wet handkerchief to cool down with.

Bring a handkerchief with you into the field. A handkerchief is a great multipurpose instrument. You can use a hanky to wipe the sweat from your brow, you can use it to catch a runny nose, you can use it to keep your head cool (as described above), and you can use it to protect your hand when holding a very hot gun barrel. After a few rounds fired, holding on to your musket can become a difficult thing, as the barrel heats up rather quickly. This is when your rifle sling becomes extremely helpful! When your barrel gets too hot to handle, just hold it by the sling as you pour your powder down the barrel, and fire it as normal.

Bring something to munch on. When you form up in your line of battle, you spend much time standing around. After a while, a few pieces of hardtack or a nice apple can be a good diversion. This is a way to keep yourself busy, as well as give you an energy boost and keeps you hydrated.

When the word comes to "fall in," get your gear, and line up with the rest of the company. Your place in line is decided by your height, for the soldiers line up "tall to small," unless you are a non-commissioned officer. Next, you count off by twos. For example, the first man is a 1, the second is a 2, the third is a 1, the fourth is a 2, etc. The twos then step back one step, and then all move over to the right. This method forms two ranks, or rows, standing at attention elbow-to-elbow, (not shoulder-to-shoulder like seen in some re-enacting units). Sometimes a unit will then drill, especially if the members are rusty after winter hibernation from the hobby, or there are some *fresh fish* (new soldiers). At your first re-

A Confederate officer prepares his men for battle. *(Courtesy of Carl Zambon)*

enactment, you will probably be made part of an *awkward squad*. This is a squad of fresh fish and seasoned veterans who do some drill on the side to acclimate the fresh fish. This way, when they take the field they will have an easier time handling their pieces and maneuvering.

One of the last things done before any unit goes out onto the battlefield, and one of the most important things as well, is the weapons inspection. If your rifle does not pass the final inspection, you will not get the green light to participate in the battle. For an inspection, the troops line up as previously described (in two ranks), but the rear rank will move back three steps when given the command. The order will then be given to fix bayonets. The men will then remove their ramrods from their rifles and place them in the barrel of their muskets, with the head (cone), or large end down. This should be one of the only times that you draw your ramrod. An officer will then go down each rank, one soldier at a time, and inspect the guns. When the officer approaches a soldier, the enlisted man presents the rifle and the officer checks the hammer and lock plate on the gun and "pings" the ramrod. He will pull the ramrod out a few inches and let it go. It should make a "pinging" sound when the head of the rammer strikes the bottom of the barrel. If it "thuds," or gets stuck in the barrel, then the rifle needs cleaning and/or maintenance. Once the inspection is complete, the soldier will then take his rifle back, and once the officer has moved on to the next inspection, will replace his ramrod in the pipes (groove) beneath the barrel. He will then place the rifle in the position of "order arms." After every gun is inspected (including small arms such as pistols), the men will then close ranks and remove bayonets. They may then be ordered to snap off a few percussion caps before further drill, just to make sure that the barrel is still clear of debris. After the inspection, the men will be ready for the battle.

Federal troops assemble for an inspection at Fort Washington National Park, Maryland. *(Photo by Robert R. Astle)*

BATTLE

The time for action has arrived! The troops are geared up, put into line, and ordered out to the front. The last few jokes are cracked as the time comes to see the elephant (Civil War slang for experiencing battle). When the line moves, you may get pushed or pulled a certain direction by a line-mate. This is just to make sure that everyone goes in the right direction and stays in their proper place. Make sure that you stay with your unit. Remember the faces around you, so that if you do get separated, you'll be able to find your place back in line. If you do get totally lost from your unit, fall in with the nearest friendly force and follow them until the conclusion of the action, or until you see a few familiar faces and can regroup with your unit. If you do end up with another organization, follow their rules and orders, and respect their officers as your own.

Federal troops mass for battle. *(Collection of Patrick A. Schroeder)*

When in battle, try to put yourself in the mindset of the 1860s Civil War soldier. Remember the tactics of the day, and do not question the officers' orders to send you straight to a grisly "death" with an unloaded rifle. Stay elbow-to-elbow, (not shoulder-to-shoulder), and make sure to fill any holes made in the front rank with men from the rear rank. The tactics of the day called for massed firepower. This was used to inflict the most damage to the enemy forces at once as quickly as possible. The enemy forces would be lined up elbow-to-elbow directly across the field, and a concentrated volley of a thousand muskets could take down hundreds of men. Battle was often a game of attrition, with whoever ran out of active battle lines of men holding their position losing the engagement.

There are no heroes during a re-enactment. Stay in line, and do not charge ahead unless ordered or scripted to. Also, remember to NEVER touch another unit's flag, especially an opposing force's flag! Fistfights have been known to erupt when, someone takes hold of another unit's flag. The re-enactors of today take much pride in their unit's colors, just like the soldiers did during the Civil War. Make sure to take pride in your colors and keep an eye out for them during the battle. Hand-to-hand combat, such as you see in the movies, is always scripted. When it comes to hand-to-hand fighting in re-enactments, it is not as glorious as in the movies, but quite easy. Just put your musket up in a guarding position across your front. Then, either you or your "opponent" will agree to take the hit (re-enactor lingo for pretending to be killed or wounded) by either nodding and/or thumping your chest, thus acknowledging that you will become the casualty in the confrontation. This is then usually followed by a phony bayonet stab, where you or your opponent will stab with your rifle as if you had your bayonet attached to it, or by crossing rifles a few times, and then taking the hit. It's easy to take a hit. Some men die dramatically, but most fall over clutching their "wound," often with a yell as they fall.

During the fight, a unit should always remember to "take hits" if the situation calls for it. If the enemy unleashes a volley of 300 muskets at you from 100 yards away and only one man takes a hit, it does not look very realistic! Use your better judgment. If an enemy soldier is looking you directly in the eyes, or in your immediate direction, and has you in his sights when he fires, take a hit. True, wind and atmospheric conditions may cause the shot to miss, but when in doubt, take a hit. The same wind and atmospheric conditions mentioned above, however, can also cause that fatal shot to become a non-mortal wound! You can always get back up and limp along right behind your lines, or walk along tenderly holding a wounded arm. If this is your first event, however, don't take a hit unless you are ordered to. You will have plenty of time to take hits in other battles.

A teamster is among the battlefield casualties. *(Collection of Patrick A. Schroeder)*

Now that you have learned how, here is how to cause others to take a hit. When loading and firing your rifle, remember safety first! Always elevate the barrel of your musket when firing, so that you are aiming above your enemies' heads. This way, nothing could fly out of the muzzle and injure someone. Always leave your *tompion* (barrel plug), in your tent before a battle. This can become a dangerous projectile. Some re-enactors do not even recommend purchasing one. Also remember to leave your ramrod in the pipes as well. A ramrod should never be drawn during battle. When priming your rifle with a percussion cap, make sure that you rest the rifle on top of your cap box. This will make sure that the barrel is elevated in case it goes off prematurely. If you are in the rear rank, make sure that the head of the soldier in front of you is safely between the second and third barrel bands of the weapon. This will protect them from the muzzle flash and noise, as well as the spark from the igniting percussion cap. Never aim directly at anyone! It is better to be safe then to be sorry. Also, never place anything in the barrel during the battle besides the black powder of the blank charge. When loading, pour the powder down the barrel, and then throw the empty cartridge paper away.

The field is littered with casualties after Confederate troops overrun a Federal artillery position and charge the reformed line. *(Collection of Patrick A. Schroeder)*

Now that you know how *not* to fire your weapon, here is the proper technique in loading your rifled musket, known as loading in nine times, taken directly from *Hardee's Rifle and Light Infantry Tactics:*

1. Load
One time and one motion.
156. Grasp the piece with the left hand as high as the right elbow, and bring it vertically opposite the middle of the body, shift the right hand to the upper band, place the butt between the feet, the barrel to the front; seize it with the left hand, near the muzzle, which should be three inches from the body; carry the right hand to the cartridge box.

2. Handle - Cartridge.
One time and one motion.
157. Seize the cartridge with the thumb and the next two fingers and place it between the teeth.

3. Tear - Cartridge.
One time and one motion.
158. Tear the paper to the powder, hold the cartridge upright

between the thumb and first two fingers, near the top; in this position place it in front of and near the muzzle-- the back of the hand to the front.

4. *Charge* - Cartridge.
One time and one motion.

159. Empty the powder into the barrel; disengage the ball from the paper with the right hand and the thumb and first two fingers of the left; insert it into the bore, the pointed end uppermost, and press it down with the right thumb; seize the head of the rammer with the thumb and fore-finger of the right hand, the other fingers closed, the elbows near the body.

5. *Draw* - Rammer.
One time and three motions.

160. (*First motion.*) Half draw the rammer by extending, the right arm; steady it in this position with the left thumb; grasp the rammer near the muzzle with the right hand, the little finger uppermost, the nails to the front, the thumb extended along the rammer.

161. (*Second motion.*) Clear the rammer from the pipes by again extending the arm; the rammer in the prolongation of the pipes.

162 (*Third motion.*) Turn the rammer, the little end of the rammer passing near the left shoulder; place the head of the rammer on the ball, the back of the hand to the front.

6. *Ram* - Cartridge.
One time and one motion.

163. Insert the rammer as far as the right, and steady it in this position with the thumb of the left hand; seize the rammer at the small end with the thumb and fore-finger of the right hand, the back of the hand to the front; press the ball home, the elbows near the body.

7. *Return.* - Rammer.
One time and three motions.

164. (*First motion.*) Draw the rammer half-way out, and steady it in this position with the left thumb; grasp it near the muzzle with the right hand, the little finger uppermost, the nails to the front, the thumb along the rammer; clear the rammer from the bore by extending the arm, the nails to the front, the rammer in the prolongation of the bore.

165. (*Second motion.*) Turn the rammer, the head of the rammer passing near the left shoulder, and insert it in the pipes until the right hand reaches the muzzle, the nails to the front.

166. (*Third motion.*) Force the rammer home by placing the little finger of the right hand on the head of the rammer; pass the left hand down

he barrel to the extent of the arm, without depressing the shoulder.

. *Prime*

One time and two motions.

167. *First motion.* With the left hand raise the piece till the hand
s as high as the eye, grasp the small of the stock with the right hand; half
ace to the right; place at the same time, the right foot behind and at right
ingles with the left; the hollow of the right foot against the left heel. Slip
he left hand down to the lower band, the thumb along the stock, the left
ilbow against the body; bring the piece to the right side, the butt below
he right fore-arm, the small of the stock against the body and two inches
)elow the right breast, the barrel upwards, the muzzle on a level with the
eye.

168. (*Second motion.*) Half cock with the thumb on the right hand,
he fingers supported against the guard and the small of the stock - remove
he old cap with one of the fingers of the right hand, and with the thumb
ind fore-finger of the same hand take a cap from the pouch, place it on the
iipple, and press it down with the thumb; seize the small of the stock with
he right hand.

). *Shoulder* - Arms.

One time and two motions.

169. (*First motion.*) Bring the piece to the right shoulder and
iupport it there with the left hand, face to the front; bring the right heel to
he side of and on a line with the left; grasp the piece with the right hand
is indicated in the position of *shoulder arms.*

170. (*Second motion.*) Drop the left hand quickly by the side.

However, when re-enacting a battle, obviously you do not follow
ill nine steps. There are six basic steps to loading in re-enacting. They
°ollow the basic structure discussed above, but with slight changes for re-
enacting:

1. Load
2. Handle - Cartridge
3. Tear - Cartridge
4. Charge - Cartridge (do not use the ramrod in this step)
5. Prime
5. Shoulder - Arms

The next steps are simple, and are well known to just about any
sid who has played army or cowboys and Indians: Ready! Aim! Fire!
Again, make sure that you aim above your intended target. Try to pay

close attention to your muzzle when you fire. This way you can be certain that the round did indeed fire. The easiest way to do this is to look for the smoke that follows each shot.

If you have trouble with your musket, don't panic! Maybe the spark from the percussion cap did not ignite the powder in the barrel, or maybe the cap fell off. Check the placement of the percussion cap first. Try firing another cap or two. Do not look down or put your face over the barrel. If problems persist, notify an officer. Then, the officer, or another member of the unit may try to address the situation. If your weapon is still malfunctioning, you will most likely be instructed to take a hit and address the problem more thoroughly back in camp. More often than not, a good cleaning will get your musket in shape for the next engagement. Sometimes, there may be a member of the unit carrying a musket beyond the rear rank for the purpose of addressing maintenance problems. If that is the case, he may take your musket from you and swap you his gun so that you may keep fighting in the battle. He will then proceed to try to clear your musket out behind the lines. If it clears after firing a few percussion caps, he will then give the musket back to you. Some units may allow young members to carry a musket, but not fire it. This way, the member can still participate in the battle without looking totally out of place, such as the under-aged color-bearers you see sometimes on the field.

The smoke hangs low during a re-enactment of the Battle of Franklin, Tennessee. *(Collection of Patrick A. Schroeder)*

(*Above*) **Troops begin to reform after the battle.** (*Below*) **Once the fighting's over, the casualties are resurrected.** (*Courtesy of Carl Zambon*)

BACK IN CAMP

No matter who wins the battle, both sides need to clean their firearms! Cleaning the rifle should be one of the first things entertained when you get back to camp. A field cleaning is a quick and easy way to make sure that you will pass the next inspection and be able to participate in the next battle. First off, boil some water (coffee works in a pinch). Then, place a rag or piece of leather under your hammer, over the touchhole in the nipple. A belt works well. Pour some of the water down the muzzle (be careful, it will heat up very quickly) and place a rag or your finger over the muzzle and rock your musket back-and-forth sloshing the hot water around in the barrel. If your belt is long enough, it can be used to cover both openings. After this is done, pour out the water—yuck! Keep repeating this procedure until the water comes out clear. Next, run a cleaning patch down the bore, using a cleaning rod, your ramrod, or an attachment to your ramrod, until these too, come out clean. Even if the water comes out clear, that patch will show you how much crud is still in the barrel! Lastly, clean the nipple out a few times with a nipple pick, and remove it with a nipple wrench and clean off some of the caked on black powder. Using this quick field cleaning system, you should be ready to go into action for the next engagement.

When you get home, you should disassemble your rifle totally and give it a thorough cleaning and oiling. Every once in a while, run a few patches down the bore. Even when you think that it is clean, you'd be surprised what you find in there after a few days. The sticking power of black powder is amazing!

After your musket is clean and ready for the next day's action, it is time to kick back, relax, and enjoy the company of your comrades. This is the time to put your feet up and chew the fat with your fellow re-enactors. Of course, the first thing to go around is everyone's opinions and personal stories of the latest battle. This is usually followed by a trip to the *sinks*, (a.k.a. porta-johns), the sutlers, or the food stands (always go for the barbecue beef sandwich)! If you go visit sutler's row, especially if you are new to the re-enacting scene, it's a good idea to bring a buddy with you. That way, you can watch out for each other when someone tries to price-gouge you, or pawn off some *farby* (non-authentic), items on new or unsuspecting re-enactors. Just because an item is sold at a sutler's tent or shop does not mean that it is period correct or authentic. A good time to visit the sutlers is during the last day of a re-enactment, after the last battle, ut before the sutlers have packed up all their wares. You can sometimes get great bargains at this time.

Nighttime is the best time to be in camp. That is when the crowds are gone, and the band-of-brother feelings kick in. That is when all the stories start going around, and when the jokes that not all spectators may appreciate can be espoused to entertain the troops. This is when the company joker pulls out his old guitar and amuses all with songs that only he can play. These are the moments that re-enactors live for; when you are one of the boys, when you forget your modern life and that you are just re-enacting, and when you cross that barrier of time and identify with the original Civil War soldiers that you are there to honor.

Recipe for Hard Tack

Ingredients:

2 cups of flour
½ to ¾ cup water
1 tbl spoon of Crisco or vegetable fat
5 pinches of salt

Mix ingredients together into a stiff batter, knead, and spread dough onto baking sheet at ½ in. thickness. Bake for ½ hour at 350 degrees. Remove from oven and cut into 3-inch squares and punch 4 rows of holes, 4 per row into the dough. Turn dough over, return to over and bake another ½ hour. Turn oven off, leave hardtack in oven until cool.

As dusk sets in, camp activities begin. *(Collection of Shaun Grenan)*

Two cold Confederate soldiers collapse after a hard fought battle. *(Courtesy of Carl Zambon)*

(Above) **Federal officers talk over the fight after the battle.** *(Below)* **General Lee is found enjoying some refreshments with local civilians.** *(Collection of Patrick A. Schroeder)*

CLEAN UP

Alas, this is it, clean up time. The worst part about Civil War re enacting is returning to the present day. Always make sure that you try to leave the campsite in the same condition when you depart, if not better than it was when you first arrived. Help your comrades pick up trash from your unit's campsite, as well as from the surrounding areas, and remember to make sure that the fire is out. It is also proper re-enactor etiquette to replace the large divot of a fire pit that your unit had dug.

When taking down your tent, make sure to remove all your gear first! It may seem like common sense, but when in a hurry, some people are prone to forget. Be sure that you help your buddies tear down and pack up their gear, just as you assisted in putting up their tents and unloading their equipment. If you help them, then they will help you, and a nice arrangement should develop for setting up and tearing down camp that will get the job done in no time at all. Re-enactors are rarely in a hurry to return to the 21st century, and part of their reason is to let the crowds disperse first. After a re-enactment concludes, there is often a mass exodus of spectators, as well as soldiers and civilians to the parking lot to hit the highway as fast as they can. This frequently causes a bottleneck and makes it take longer for everyone to get home. This is a good time to pack up all your gear, except the camp stools and beverages, and then you can you sit around shooting the breeze or look for that last-minute sale at the sutlers. This can be a time to slowly ease back into the present-time frame of mind, whilst reviewing the happenings of the day or of the entire event. It is also a good time to bring up the next event, or to throw around ideas picked-up over the weekend. Sometimes, units may use this time for a short meeting or to discuss topics or problems that have arisen from the past weekend. It is then time for a few hardy parting handshakes and good-byes until the next event (which is never that far away, even though it may feel it). This is when you realize if the weekend was truly fulfilling.

The ride back may seem a bit somber. The journey often feels longer that it really is, but again, your fellow car-mates can always engage the party in discussions about various incidents from the latest re-enactment, or re-fight the battle just like old veterans. The stories will often encompass the entire ride home. The energy and liveliness from the ride down to the event may be gone, but the spark that created them is still evident. You may even breathe a sigh of relief, as you can't wait to tell all your friends or coworkers of your latest exploits. One thing is certain, for many, re-enacting is the best hobby out there!

APPENDIX 1: BASIC DRILL MADE EASY

Reading and learning even the most basic drill of the Civil War re-enactor can be a chore. The Victorian style of writing contributes to that. This next section is an attempt to give the "fresh fish" knowledge of the basic motions and maneuvers of infantry drill before they set out on the field. We'll look at the drill at a company level. A regiment was to be composed of ten companies (labeled A, B, C, D, E, F, G, H, I, and K)—there was no J company—each composed of 100 men. On paper, a full regiment would number around 1,000 men.

Attention - Company! You will often hear this command a lot in the field. The first command, **attention**, is a preparatory command. This is to ready you for the next command. The second command is the action command. That is the command on which you actually move. On *company*, the men should all come to the position of attention, which is standing up straight with your arms at your sides, with your little fingers along the seams of your trousers. Make sure to bend your knees slightly—do not lock your knees! Your eyes should be focused straight ahead, and there should be no talking. You should be standing elbow-to-elbow with the men/man next to you, and if you are in the second rank, you should be about 13 inches from the knapsack of the man in front of you. The easiest way to do this is to put your arm at your side and then raise your forearm with your hand extended, forming a right angle at your elbow. The tips of your extended fingers should touch the back of the man in front of you. The rear rank should always be forearm distance from the front rank to assure a compact, sharp-looking body of troops.

Order - Arms! When in the position of *attention* and carrying a rifle, you should have the rifle in the position of *order arms*. To do so, place the rifle butt on the ground, trigger outwards, in the crook of your right arm. Place your right hand on the side of the gun to steady it, and keep your left hand at your side.

Shoulder - Arms! This is naturally the next command when handling rifles. From the position of *order arms*, use your right hand to grasp the musket and lift it up to your right shoulder, keeping the trigger outwards. Then take your left hand and grab the rifle and hold it at the bottom band. Next, place your right hand, with the index finger curved under the trigger guard. Make sure to also wrap your thumb around the trigger guard. Let the weight of the rifle settle on your finger and against your arm. The last step is to place your left hand at your side. To go from *shoulder arms* back to *order arms*, just do all of the steps in reverse. All other movements start and return to *shoulder arms*; thus it is known as the "position of the soldier."

     Right Shoulder Shift - Arms! This is a common order heard on the march. When marching at the double quick (a slight jogging pace, but not a run), you will also use this position. From *shoulder arms*, lift the rifle up with your right index finger so the trigger is pointing outward near your shoulder. Turn the gun while doing this so that the trigger is pointing toward your neck. Next grab the small of the stock with your left hand and hold the gun while you place your right hand palm up under the butt plate of the rifle. Make certain to keep the elbow of your right hand close to your body, and place your left arm at your side. The stock of the rifle should be resting on your collarbone. If it hurts, then you are doing it right (a common re-enactor saying). If you are at *right shoulder shift* while marching, and the order to *halt* is given, always remember to go immediately to *shoulder arms*. The order will not be given—it is just something that you will have to remember to do.

     Support - Arms! This is another position used while marching and while on guard duty. From the position of *shoulder arms*, move the rifle with your right hand so that it is directly out in front of you. It should be lined up directly in line with your nose. Next grasp the rifle with your left hand at the bottom band and turn the rifle so that the trigger is pointing towards you. Place your right hand under the butt of the rifle and lift it so that the trigger is in the crook of your left arm. Bend your left arm over the gun so that the hammer is resting on your forearm, which should be drawn close to your body. Finally place your right hand at your side. This is often a preferred method to carry a rifle for long periods of time because it gives your right arm and shoulder a break. If, when marching at *support arms*, the command *"Rest"* is given, you are to place your right hand at the small of the stock and keep your elbow close to your body.

     Trail - Arms! If you end up marching under branches or in a spot where you need to keep your rifle low, this command will be given. Take the position of *order arms*, but do not place your rifle butt on the ground. Keep the rifle a few inches off the ground and tilt the muzzle of the rifle forward at about a 45-degree angle. If you have a bayonet attached, you will probably want to use a smaller angle, especially if you are in the rear rank. Always remember to watch out for the man in front of you! It is also important to remember, when returning to the *shoulder arms*, and the preparatory command *shoulder* is given to **straighten** the muzzle of your weapon back to 90 degrees. This small detail is overlooked by many units in the hobby.

Secure - *Arms!* This position is not used very often, but is important to learn nonetheless. It is used in cemetery processions, as well as during rainy weather, to keep the mechanics of the musket dry. From *shoulder arms*, go to the position of *support arms*, but do not cross your left arm over to balance the hammer on. Instead, grab the musket over the bottom band with your left hand, and place your thumb over the shaft of the ramrod. Tilt the musket muzzle towards the ground and make sure the lock-plate is in your armpit. The hammer should be pointing towards the ground with the barrel at close to a 45-degree angle.

Present - *Arms!* This is a soldier's salute with his weapon while in ranks. From *shoulder arms*, move the rifle out in front of you with your right hand so that it is parallel with your nose. Next, grab the rifle with your left hand at the lower band, and grab the small of the stock with your right hand. The middle band should be even with your eyes.

These are the basic elements of drill that you will use over and over again. This is also commonly known as the ***Manual of Arms***. If you know this drill before your first event, it will be much easier to follow the commands and fit in with veterans of the hobby.

Federal re-enactors construct breastworks anticipating a Confederate attack.
(Collection of Patrick A. Schroeder)

APPENDIX 2: GLOSSARY OF TERMS

Accoutrements - The basic equipment of the soldier, such as a belt, cartridge box, cap box, bayonet scabbard, canteen, etc.

Action Command - The part of an order on which you actually move. This follows a preparatory command.

Awkward Squad - Squad of new recruits and veterans who drill for the practice and teaching of the "fresh fish."

Bayonet - Piercing blade attached to the muzzle of a rifle or musket.

Blanket Roll - A blanket rolled up, folded over the shoulder, and tied on the end, near the hip. Often extra clothing or possessions are rolled up inside.

Blouse - Another name for the sack coat.

Brogans - Leather shoes with pegged or stitched on soles. They often have metal plates nailed to the heels for added durability.

Bummer - Nickname for a forage cap.

Butt plate - Metal plate over the butt end of your rifle.

Cap Box - Leather pouch worn on belt that holds percussion caps.

Carbine - Short barreled rifle for use by mounted troops.

Cartridge Box - Leather pouch worn on a sling over the left shoulder, or on the belt, that holds rounds for your weapon. Some contain pockets to hold gun tools.

Color Bearer - A unit's flag carrier.

Cleaning Patch - Small piece of cloth rammed down the barrel of gun to remove residue from inside the barrel.

Chasseurs - Troops whose uniform is based on the French Light Infantry, or *Chasseurs a Pied.*

Enfield - More common name for the .577 caliber Enfield rifled-musket or one of its copies.

FARB - Acronym for Fallacious Accoutrements and Reprehensible Baggage. There are many explanations for the origin of this word. One of them apparently stems from Civil War use, as seen in a soldier's letter home. Synonymous with fake and unauthentic.

Farby - Not authentic or period correct.

Forage Cap - High crowned visored cap with a floppy body and a leather chinstrap affixed by two brass buttons. Some enlisted men decorated their caps with brass letters, numbers, or badges.

Fresh Fish - A new recruit/re-enactor.

Frock Coat – Lower-thigh-length uniform coat usually worn for dress occasions, but was the regulation battle wear of the Union army. It has a standing collar and usually closed with a 9-button front.

Frog - Leather accoutrement for holding the bayonet scabbard to the belt.

Hard-core – Campaigning, progressive re-enactors who are as authentic in their impressions as possible. Often they sleep on the ground in the open and only eat food available to soldiers in the Civil War. This is a growing faction of the re-enacting community.

Hammer - The metal lever on a gun that strikes down on a percussion cap when the trigger is pulled.

Hardee Hat - Model 1858 black felt dress hat with a stiff brim and crown. These were quite unpopular with most troops, outside the Iron Brigade.

Hussars - Units resembling one type of European light cavalry regiments.

Haversack - Cloth or painted or tarred-cloth bag for carrying rations and personal belongings worn over the right shoulder. Flap opening closes with a buckle or buttons.

Kepi - Low crowned cap, resembling a forage cap, but is shorter and more compact.

Leathers - The belt, cap box, and cartridge box.

Mule Collar - Nickname for a blanket roll.

Muzzle - Opening of the gun barrel.

Lock Plate - Metal plate on the side of your rifle that has the mechanics of the gun attached to the backside. Often has the makers' stamp on it.

Nipple - Metal cone-shaped piece on a gun that you place a percussion cap on when firing.

Ping - The sound you should hear when the ramrod is dropped down the barrel. Hearing this sound should mean that your rifle is clean.

Ramrod - Metal pole kept in sheath (groove) under gun barrel that is used to ram a charge down the barrel.

Prepatory Command - In an order, used to ready the men for a forthcoming command.

Sack Coat - Loose-fitting uniform coat with a pocket and usually four buttons. Officially to be used in fatigue duty. Meant to reach slightly below the hips.

Scabbard - Sheath for a bayonet or sword.

Shelter Half - Half of a dog tent, measuring 4¾' x 4¾'. A soldier would button his half to another soldier's half to form a tent for two men.

Shell Jacket – A tight fitting, nine button uniform jacket.

Sinks - The bathrooms or port-a-johns.

Sutler - Originally a person who sold goods to the soldiers that they were not issued or could not easy obtain. Now, a person or business that sells or makes re-enacting goods.

Taking a Hit - Becoming a casualty.

Testament - A small pocket Bible often carried by soldiers.

Tins - Metal inserts for a cartridge box that hold cartridges.

Tompion - Muzzle plug for a gun.

Toothpick - Nickname for a large, wicked-looking knife carried by soldiers.

Vivandiere - A woman wearing military garb in the style of their regiment who accompanied a Zouave regiment. They sometimes would act as sutlers and nurses.

Worm - Screw-shaped metal device for removing obstructions from a gun barrel. Also called a wiper.

Zouaves - Units whose uniforms and/or drill are based on French infantry who adopted them from an Algerian tribe, the Zouaoua.

The 114th Pennsylvania Collis' Zouaves, pose with their Vivandiere. *(Collection of Shaun Grenan)*

BIBLIOGRAPHY

Davis, W. J. & Pritchard, R., *Battlefields of the Civil War.* Thunder Bay Press, 1999.

Davis, W. J. & Pritchard, R., *Fighting Men of the Civil War.* Thunder Bay Press, 1998.

Hardee, Brevet Lt. W. J., *Hardee's Rifle and Light Infantry Tactics.* Philadelphia, PA, 1855.

McAfee, Michael J., *Zouaves: The First and the Bravest.* Gettysburg, PA: Thomas Publications, 1991.

Time Life, Inc., *Echoes of Glory: Arms and Equipment of the Confederacy.* Alexandria, VA: Time Life Books, Ed.1992.

Time Life, Inc., *Echoes of Glory: Arms and Equipment of the Union.* Alexandria, VA: Time Life Books, Ed. 1992.

Tucker, Glen. *High Tide at Gettysburg.* Gettysburg, PA: Stan Clark Military Books, 1995. p. 364.

SUGGESTED READING

For further reading on the great hobby of Civil War re-enacting, as well as the Civil War in general, check out these great books:

- *A Duryée Zouave*, by Thomas P. Southwick
- *All For the Union*, by Elisha Hunt Rhodes
- *American Civil War Armies Series*, by Osprey Military Books
- *American Civil War Zouaves*, by Robin Smith and Bill Younghusband
- *Andersonville Diary* by John Ranson
- *Battle Cry of Freedom*, by James McPherson
- *Campaigning With Grant* by Horace Porter
- *Civil War Soldier Life: In Camp and Battle*, by George F. Williams
- *Co. Aytch*, by Sam Watkins
- *Detailed Minutia of Soldier Life* by Carlton McCarthy
- *Grand Re-enactments of an Anguished Time,* by Kent Courtney and R. Lee Haddon
- *Hardtack and Coffee*, by John D. Billings
- *Infantryman*, by Gregory A. Coco
- *Mosby's Men* by John Alexander
- *One of Jackson's Foot Cavalry* by John H. Worsham
- *Passing of the Armies* by Joshua L. Chamberlain
- *Re-enactors' Guide to Black Powder*, by David Smith
- *Reminiscences of the Civil War* by John B. Gordon
- *Soldiers in America*, by Don Troiani
- *Thirty Myths of Lee's Surrender*, by Patrick A. Schroeder
- *Three Months in the Southern States,* by Arthur Fremantle
- We *Came To Fight*, by Patrick A. Schroeder

ABOUT THE AUTHOR

Photograph by R. J. Gibson

Shaun C. Grenan was born in Detroit, Michigan, in 1980. His interest in the Civil War began in grade school, and was furthered by all the books and frequent trips to the library that his mother provided him. In 2000, Shaun fulfilled his dream of moving to Gettysburg, Pennsylvania, to live and work in a historical setting. Shaun re-enacts with the 114th Pennsylvania Volunteer Infantry, *Collis' Zouaves*. He also portrays Colonel Elmer Ellsworth of the 11th New York Volunteer Infantry (the 1st New York Fire Zouaves) for living history and historical presentations. He has recently organized the United States Zouave Battalion, an organization of Union Zouave re-enacting units.

Grenan's special areas of study focus on Civil War Zouaves and Elmer Ellsworth. He hopes to tackle both subjects in future publications. His websites may be found at:

Civil War Zouaves -- www.zouavedatabase.org
114th Pennsylvania Re-enactors -- http://144thpa.tripod.com
United States Zouave Battalion -- www.geocities.com/zouavebattalion

For a complete book and price list write:

SCHROEDER PUBLICATIONS
131 Tanglewood Drive, Lynchburg, VA 24502
www.civilwar-books.com
Email: civilwarbooks@yahoo.com

Titles Available:

* **The Pennsylvania Bucktails: A Photographic Album of the 42nd, 149th & 150th Pennsylvania Regiments** by Patrick A. Schroeder ISBN 1-889246-14-X

* **Thirty Myths About Lee's Surrender** by Patrick A. Schroeder
  ISBN 1-889246-05-0

* **More Myths About Lee's Surrender** by Patrick A. Schroeder
  ISBN 1-889246-01-8

* **The Confederate Cemetery at Appomattox** by Patrick A. Schroeder
  ISBN 1-889246-11-5

* **Recollections & Reminiscences of Old Appomattox and Its People**
  by George T. Peers ISBN 1-889246-12-3

* **Tar Heels: Five Points in the Record of North Carolina in the Great War of 1861-5**
  by the Committee appointed by the North Carolina Literary and Historical
  Society ISBN 1-889246-02-6 (Soft cover) ISBN 1-889246-15-8 (Hard cover)

* **The Fighting Quakers** by A. J. H. Duganne ISBN 1-889246-03-4

* **A Duryée Zouave** by Thomas P. Southwick ISBN 1-56190-086-9 (Soft cover)
  ISBN 1-889246-24-7 (Hard Cover)

* **Civil War Soldier Life: In Camp and Battle** by George F. Williams
  ISBN 1-889246-04-2

* **We Came To Fight: The History of the 5th New York Veteran Volunteer Infantry, Duryée's Zouaves, (1863-1865)** by Patrick A. Schroeder ISBN 1-889246-07-7

* **A Swedish Officer in the American Civil War: The Diary of Axel Leatz of the 5th New York Veteran Volunteer Infantry, Duryée's Zouaves, (1863-1865)** edited by Patrick A. Schroeder ISBN 1-889246-06-9

* **Campaigns of the 146th Regiment New York State Volunteers**
  by Mary Genevie Green Brainard ISBN 1-889246-08-5

* **The Highest Praise of Gallantry: Memorials of David T. & James E. Jenkins**
  by A. Pierson Case and New Material by Patrick Schroeder ISBN 1-889246-17-4

* **Where Duty Called them: The Story of the Samuel Babcock Family of Homer, New York, in the Civil War** ISBN1-889246-49-2

* **The Bloody 85th: The Letters of Milton McJunkin, A Western Pennsylvania Soldier in the Civil War** edited by Richard A. Sauers, Ronn Palm, and Patrick A. Schroeder
  ISBN 1-889246-13-1 (Soft cover) ISBN 1-889246-16-6 (Hard cover)